AVERNO

AVERNO

LOUISE GLÜCK

FARRAR, STRAUS AND GIROUX

NEW YORK

Farrar, Straus and Giroux
19 Union Square West, New York 10003

Distributed in Canada by Douglas & McIntyre Ltd.
Printed in the United States of America
First edition, 2006

Grateful acknowledgment is made to the following publications, in whose pages these
poems first appeared: The New Yorker, The New York Times, Poetry ("Archaic Fragment,"
"Averno," and "The Evening Star"), The Threepenny Review, Triquarterly, and Slate.

"October" was originally printed by Sarabande Books as a chapbook in 2004.

"Omens" originally appeared in After Pushkin (Carcanet Press Ltd., 1999).

Library of Congress Cataloging-in-Publication Data
Glück, Louise, 1943–
    Averno / Louise Glück.—1st ed.
      p. cm.
    ISBN-13: 978-0-374-10742-0 (alk. paper)
    ISBN-10: 0-374-10742-4 (alk. paper)
    1. Persephone (Greek deity)—Poetry.   I. Title.

  PS3557.L8A96 2006
  811'.54—dc22

                       2005042658

www.fsgbooks.com

10 9 8 7 6 5 4 3 2

for Noah

CONTENTS

AVERNO

Averno. Ancient name Avernus. A small crater lake, ten miles west of Naples, Italy; regarded by the ancient Romans as the entrance to the underworld.

THE NIGHT MIGRATIONS

This is the moment when you see again
the red berries of the mountain ash
and in the dark sky
the birds' night migrations.

It grieves me to think
the dead won't see them—
these things we depend on,
they disappear.

What will the soul do for solace then?
I tell myself maybe it won't need
these pleasures anymore;
maybe just not being is simply enough,
hard as that is to imagine.

I

OCTOBER

I.

Is it winter again, is it cold again,
didn't Frank just slip on the ice,
didn't he heal, weren't the spring seeds planted

didn't the night end,
didn't the melting ice
flood the narrow gutters

wasn't my body
rescued, wasn't it safe

didn't the scar form, invisible
above the injury

terror and cold,
didn't they just end, wasn't the back garden
harrowed and planted—

I remember how the earth felt, red and dense,
in stiff rows, weren't the seeds planted,
didn't vines climb the south wall

I can't hear your voice
for the wind's cries, whistling over the bare ground

I no longer care
what sound it makes

when was I silenced, when did it first seem
pointless to describe that sound

what it sounds like can't change what it is—

didn't the night end, wasn't the earth
safe when it was planted

didn't we plant the seeds,
weren't we necessary to the earth,

the vines, were they harvested?

2.

Summer after summer has ended,
balm after violence:
it does me no good
to be good to me now;
violence has changed me.

Daybreak. The low hills shine
ochre and fire, even the fields shine.
I know what I see; sun that could be
the August sun, returning
everything that was taken away—

You hear this voice? This is my mind's voice;
you can't touch my body now.
It has changed once, it has hardened,
don't ask it to respond again.

A day like a day in summer.
Exceptionally still. The long shadows of the maples
nearly mauve on the gravel paths.
And in the evening, warmth. Night like a night in summer.

It does me no good; violence has changed me.
My body has grown cold like the stripped fields;
now there is only my mind, cautious and wary,
with the sense it is being tested.

Once more, the sun rises as it rose in summer;
bounty, balm after violence.
Balm after the leaves have changed, after the fields
have been harvested and turned.

Tell me this is the future,
I won't believe you.
Tell me I'm living,
I won't believe you.

3.

Snow had fallen. I remember
music from an open window.

Come to me, said the world.
This is not to say
it spoke in exact sentences
but that I perceived beauty in this manner.

Sunrise. A film of moisture
on each living thing. Pools of cold light
formed in the gutters.

I stood
at the doorway,
ridiculous as it now seems.

What others found in art,
I found in nature. What others found
in human love, I found in nature.
Very simple. But there was no voice there.

Winter was over. In the thawed dirt,
bits of green were showing.

Come to me, said the world. I was standing
in my wool coat at a kind of bright portal—
I can finally say
long ago; it gives me considerable pleasure. Beauty

the healer, the teacher—

death cannot harm me
more than you have harmed me,
my beloved life.

4.

The light has changed;
middle C is tuned darker now.
And the songs of morning sound over-rehearsed.

This is the light of autumn, not the light of spring.
The light of autumn: *you will not be spared.*

The songs have changed; the unspeakable
has entered them.

This is the light of autumn, not the light that says
I am reborn.

Not the spring dawn: *I strained, I suffered, I was delivered.*
This is the present, an allegory of waste.

So much has changed. And still, you are fortunate:
the ideal burns in you like a fever.
Or not like a fever, like a second heart.

The songs have changed, but really they are still quite beautiful.
They have been concentrated in a smaller space, the space of the mind.
They are dark, now, with desolation and anguish.

And yet the notes recur. They hover oddly
in anticipation of silence.
The ear gets used to them.
The eye gets used to disappearances.

You will not be spared, nor will what you love be spared.

A wind has come and gone, taking apart the mind;
it has left in its wake a strange lucidity.

How privileged you are, to be still passionately
clinging to what you love;
the forfeit of hope has not destroyed you.

Maestoso, doloroso:

This is the light of autumn; it has turned on us.
Surely it is a privilege to approach the end
still believing in something.

5.

It is true there is not enough beauty in the world.
It is also true that I am not competent to restore it.
Neither is there candor, and here I may be of some use.

I am
at work, though I am silent.

The bland

misery of the world
bounds us on either side, an alley

lined with trees; we are

companions here, not speaking,
each with his own thoughts;

behind the trees, iron
gates of the private houses,
the shuttered rooms

somehow deserted, abandoned,

as though it were the artist's
duty to create
hope, but out of what? what?

the word itself
false, a device to refute
perception— At the intersection,

ornamental lights of the season.

I was young here. Riding
the subway with my small book
as though to defend myself against

this same world:

you are not alone,
the poem said,
in the dark tunnel.

6.

The brightness of the day becomes
the brightness of the night;
the fire becomes the mirror.

My friend the earth is bitter; I think
sunlight has failed her.
Bitter or weary, it is hard to say.

Between herself and the sun,
something has ended.
She wants, now, to be left alone;
I think we must give up
turning to her for affirmation.

Above the fields,
above the roofs of the village houses,
the brilliance that made all life possible
becomes the cold stars.

Lie still and watch:
they give nothing but ask nothing.

From within the earth's
bitter disgrace, coldness and barrenness

my friend the moon rises:
she is beautiful tonight, but when is she not beautiful?

PERSEPHONE THE WANDERER

In the first version, Persephone
is taken from her mother
and the goddess of the earth
punishes the earth—this is
consistent with what we know of human behavior,

that human beings take profound satisfaction
in doing harm, particularly
unconscious harm:

we may call this
negative creation.

Persephone's initial
sojourn in hell continues to be
pawed over by scholars who dispute
the sensations of the virgin:

did she cooperate in her rape,
or was she drugged, violated against her will,
as happens so often now to modern girls.

As is well known, the return of the beloved
does not correct
the loss of the beloved: Persephone

returns home
stained with red juice like
a character in Hawthorne—

I am not certain I will
keep this word: is earth
"home" to Persephone? Is she at home, conceivably,
in the bed of the god? Is she
at home nowhere? Is she
a born wanderer, in other words
an existential
replica of her own mother, less
hamstrung by ideas of causality?

You are allowed to like
no one, you know. The characters
are not people.
They are aspects of a dilemma or conflict.

Three parts: just as the soul is divided,
ego, superego, id. Likewise

the three levels of the known world,
a kind of diagram that separates
heaven from earth from hell.

You must ask yourself:
where is it snowing?

White of forgetfulness,
of desecration—

It is snowing on earth; the cold wind says

Persephone is having sex in hell.
Unlike the rest of us, she doesn't know
what winter is, only that
she is what causes it.

She is lying in the bed of Hades.
What is in her mind?
Is she afraid? Has something
blotted out the idea
of mind?

She does know the earth
is run by mothers, this much
is certain. She also knows
she is not what is called
a girl any longer. Regarding
incarceration, she believes

she has been a prisoner since she has been a daughter.

The terrible reunions in store for her
will take up the rest of her life.
When the passion for expiation
is chronic, fierce, you do not choose
the way you live. You do not live;
you are not allowed to die.

You drift between earth and death
which seem, finally,
strangely alike. Scholars tell us

that there is no point in knowing what you want
when the forces contending over you
could kill you.

White of forgetfulness,
white of safety—

They say
there is a rift in the human soul
which was not constructed to belong
entirely to life. Earth

asks us to deny this rift, a threat
disguised as suggestion—
as we have seen
in the tale of Persephone
which should be read

as an argument between the mother and the lover—
the daughter is just meat.

When death confronts her, she has never seen
the meadow without the daisies.
Suddenly she is no longer
singing her maidenly songs
about her mother's
beauty and fecundity. Where
the rift is, the break is.

Song of the earth,
song of the mythic vision of eternal life—

My soul
shattered with the strain
of trying to belong to earth—

What will you do,
when it is your turn in the field with the god?

PRISM

1.

Who can say what the world is? The world
is in flux, therefore
unreadable, the winds shifting,
the great plates invisibly shifting and changing—

2.

Dirt. Fragments
of blistered rock. On which
the exposed heart constructs
a house, memory: the gardens
manageable, small in scale, the beds
damp at the sea's edge—

3.

As one takes in
an enemy, through these windows
one takes in
the world:

here is the kitchen, here the darkened study.

Meaning: I am master here.

4.

When you fall in love, my sister said,
it's like being struck by lightning.

She was speaking hopefully,
to draw the attention of the lightning.

I reminded her that she was repeating exactly
our mother's formula, which she and I

had discussed in childhood, because we both felt
that what we were looking at in the adults

were the effects not of lightning
but of the electric chair.

5.
Riddle:
Why was my mother happy?

Answer:
She married my father.

6.
"You girls," my mother said, "should marry
someone like your father."

That was one remark. Another was,
"There is no one like your father."

7.
From the pierced clouds, steady lines of silver.

Unlikely
yellow of the witch hazel, veins
of mercury that were the paths of the rivers—

Then the rain again, erasing
footprints in the damp earth.

An implied path, like
a map without a crossroads.

8.
The implication was, it was necessary to abandon
childhood. The word "marry" was a signal.
You could also treat it as aesthetic advice;
the voice of the child was tiresome,
it had no lower register.
The word was a code, mysterious, like the Rosetta stone.
It was also a roadsign, a warning.
You could take a few things with you like a dowry.
You could take the part of you that thought.
"Marry" meant you should keep that part quiet.

9.
A night in summer. Outside,
sounds of a summer storm. Then the sky clearing.
In the window, constellations of summer.

I'm in a bed. This man and I,
we are suspended in the strange calm
sex often induces. Most sex induces.
Longing, what is that? Desire, what is that?

In the window, constellations of summer.
Once, I could name them.

10.
Abstracted
shapes, patterns.
The light of the mind. The cold, exacting
fires of disinterestedness, curiously

blocked by earth, coherent, glittering
in air and water,

the elaborate
signs that said *now plant, now harvest*—

I could name them, I had names for them:
two different things.

11.
Fabulous things, stars.

When I was a child, I suffered from insomnia.
Summer nights, my parents permitted me to sit by the lake;
I took the dog for company.

Did I say "suffered"? That was my parents' way of explaining
tastes that seemed to them
inexplicable: better "suffered" than "preferred to live with the dog."

Darkness. Silence that annulled mortality.
The tethered boats rising and falling.
When the moon was full, I could sometimes read the girls' names
painted to the sides of the boats:
Ruth Ann, Sweet Izzy, Peggy My Darling—

They were going nowhere, those girls.
There was nothing to be learned from them.

I spread my jacket in the damp sand,
the dog curled up beside me.
My parents couldn't see the life in my head;
when I wrote it down, they fixed the spelling.

Sounds of the lake. The soothing, inhuman
sounds of water lapping the dock, the dog scuffling somewhere
in the weeds—

12.
The assignment was to fall in love.
The details were up to you.
The second part was
to include in the poem certain words,
words drawn from a specific text
on another subject altogether.

13.
Spring rain, then a night in summer.
A man's voice, then a woman's voice.

You grew up, you were struck by lightning.
When you opened your eyes, you were wired forever to your true love.

It only happened once. Then you were taken care of,
your story was finished.

It happened once. Being struck was like being vaccinated;
the rest of your life you were immune,
you were warm and dry.

Unless the shock wasn't deep enough.
Then you weren't vaccinated, you were addicted.

14.
The assignment was to fall in love.
The author was female.
The ego had to be called the soul.

The action took place in the body.
Stars represented everything else: dreams, the mind, etc.

The beloved was identified
with the self in a narcissistic projection.
The mind was a subplot. It went nattering on.

Time was experienced
less as narrative than ritual.
What was repeated had weight.

Certain endings were tragic, thus acceptable.
Everything else was failure.

15.
Deceit. Lies. Embellishments we call
hypotheses—

There were too many roads, too many versions.
There were too many roads, no one path—

And at the end?

16.
List the implications of "crossroads."

Answer: a story that will have a moral.

Give a counter-example:

17.
The self ended and the world began.
They were of equal size,
commensurate,
one mirrored the other.

18.
The riddle was: why couldn't we live in the mind.

The answer was: the barrier of the earth intervened.

19.
The room was quiet.
That is, the room was quiet, but the lovers were breathing.

In the same way, the night was dark.
It was dark, but the stars shone.

The man in bed was one of several men
to whom I gave my heart. The gift of the self,
that is without limit.
Without limit, though it recurs.

The room was quiet. It was an absolute,
like the black night.

20.
A night in summer. Sounds of a summer storm.
The great plates invisibly shifting and changing—

And in the dark room, the lovers sleeping in each other's arms.

We are, each of us, the one who wakens first,
who stirs first and sees, there in the first dawn,
the stranger.

CRATER LAKE

There was a war between good and evil.
We decided to call the body good.

That made death evil.
It turned the soul
against death completely.

Like a foot soldier wanting
to serve a great warrior, the soul
wanted to side with the body.

It turned against the dark,
against the forms of death
it recognized.

Where does the voice come from
that says suppose the war
is evil, that says

suppose the body did this to us,
made us afraid of love—

ECHOES

I.

Once I could imagine my soul
I could imagine my death.
When I imagined my death
my soul died. This
I remember clearly.

My body persisted.
Not thrived, but persisted.
Why I do not know.

2.

When I was still very young
my parents moved to a small valley
surrounded by mountains
in what was called the lake country.
From our kitchen garden
you could see the mountains,
snow covered, even in summer.

I remember peace of a kind
I never knew again.

Somewhat later, I took it upon myself
to become an artist,
to give voice to these impressions.

3.
The rest I have told you already.
A few years of fluency, and then
the long silence, like the silence in the valley
before the mountains send back
your own voice changed to the voice of nature.

This silence is my companion now.
I ask: *of what did my soul die?*
and the silence answers

if your soul died, whose life
are you living and
when did you become that person?

FUGUE

1.
I was the man because I was taller.
My sister decided
when we should eat.
From time to time, she'd have a baby.

2.
Then my soul appeared.
Who are you, I said.
And my soul said,
I am your soul, the winsome stranger.

3.
Our dead sister
waited, undiscovered in my mother's head.
Our dead sister was neither
a man nor a woman. She was like a soul.

4.
My soul was taken in:
it attached itself to a man.
Not a real man, the man
I pretended to be, playing with my sister.

5.
It is coming back to me—lying on the couch
has refreshed my memory.
My memory is like a basement filled with old papers:
nothing ever changes.

6.

I had a dream: my mother fell out of a tree.
After she fell, the tree died:
it had outlived its function.
My mother was unharmed—her arrows disappeared, her wings
turned into arms. Fire creature: Sagittarius. She finds herself in—

a suburban garden. It is coming back to me.

7.

I put the book aside. What is a soul?
A flag flown
too high on the pole, if you know what I mean.

The body
cowers in the dreamlike underbrush.

8.

Well, we are here to do something about that.

(In a German accent.)

9.

I had a dream: we are at war.
My mother leaves her crossbow in the high grass.

(Sagittarius, the archer.)

My childhood, closed to me forever,
turned gold like an autumn garden,
mulched with a thick layer of salt marsh hay.

10.
A golden bow: a useful gift in wartime.

How heavy it was—no child could pick it up.

Except me: I could pick it up.

11.
Then I was wounded. The bow
was now a harp, its string cutting
deep into my palm. In the dream

it both makes the wound and seals the wound.

12.
My childhood: closed to me. Or is it
under the mulch—fertile.

But very dark. Very hidden.

13.
In the dark, my soul said
I am your soul.

No one can see me; only you—
only you can see me.

14.
And it said, you must trust me.

Meaning: if you move the harp,
you will bleed to death.

15.
Why can't I cry out?

I should be writing *my hand is bleeding,*
feeling pain and terror—what
I felt in the dream, as a casualty of war.

16.
It is coming back to me.

Pear tree. Apple tree.

I used to sit there
pulling arrows out of my heart.

17.
Then my soul appeared. It said
just as no one can see me, no one
can see the blood.

Also: no one can see the harp.

Then it said
I can save you. Meaning
this is a test.

18.
Who is "you"? As in

"Are you tired of invisible pain?"

19.
Like a small bird sealed off from daylight:

that was my childhood.

20.
I was the man because I was taller.

But I wasn't tall—
didn't I ever look in a mirror?

21.
Silence in the nursery,
the consulting garden. Then:

What does the harp suggest?

22.
I know what you want—
you want Orpheus, you want death.

Orpheus who said "Help me find Eurydice."

Then the music began, the lament of the soul
watching the body vanish.

II

THE EVENING STAR

Tonight, for the first time in many years,
there appeared to me again
a vision of the earth's splendor:

in the evening sky
the first star seemed
to increase in brilliance
as the earth darkened

until at last it could grow no darker.
And the light, which was the light of death,
seemed to restore to earth

its power to console. There were
no other stars. Only the one
whose name I knew

as in my other life I did her
injury: Venus,
star of the early evening,

to you I dedicate
my vision, since on this blank surface

you have cast enough light
to make my thought
visible again.

LANDSCAPE

I.

The sun is setting behind the mountains,
the earth is cooling.
A stranger has tied his horse to a bare chestnut tree.
The horse is quiet—he turns his head suddenly,
hearing, in the distance, the sound of the sea.

I make my bed for the night here,
spreading my heaviest quilt over the damp earth.

The sound of the sea—
when the horse turns its head, I can hear it.

On a path through the bare chestnut trees,
a little dog trails its master.

The little dog—didn't he used to rush ahead,
straining the leash, as though to show his master
what he sees there, there in the future—

the future, the path, call it what you will.

Behind the trees, at sunset, it is as though a great fire
is burning between two mountains
so that the snow on the highest precipice
seems, for a moment, to be burning also.

Listen: at the path's end the man is calling out.
His voice has become very strange now,
the voice of a person calling to what he can't see.

Over and over he calls out among the dark chestnut trees.
Until the animal responds
faintly, from a great distance,
as though this thing we fear
were not terrible.

Twilight: the stranger has untied his horse.

The sound of the sea—
just memory now.

2.

Time passed, turning everything to ice.
Under the ice, the future stirred.
If you fell into it, you died.

It was a time
of waiting, of suspended action.

I lived in the present, which was
that part of the future you could see.
The past floated above my head,
like the sun and moon, visible but never reachable.

It was a time
governed by contradictions, as in
I felt nothing and
I was afraid.

Winter emptied the trees, filled them again with snow.
Because I couldn't feel, snow fell, the lake froze over.
Because I was afraid, I didn't move;
my breath was white, a description of silence.

Time passed, and some of it became this.
And some of it simply evaporated;
you could see it float above the white trees
forming particles of ice.

All your life, you wait for the propitious time.
Then the propitious time
reveals itself as action taken.

I watched the past move, a line of clouds moving
from left to right or right to left,
depending on the wind. Some days

there was no wind. The clouds seemed
to stay where they were,
like a painting of the sea, more still than real.

Some days the lake was a sheet of glass.
Under the glass, the future made
demure, inviting sounds:
you had to tense yourself so as not to listen.

Time passed; you got to see a piece of it.
The years it took with it were years of winter;
they would not be missed. Some days

there were no clouds, as though
the sources of the past had vanished. The world

was bleached, like a negative; the light passed
directly through it. Then
the image faded.

Above the world
there was only blue, blue everywhere.

3.

In late autumn a young girl set fire to a field
of wheat. The autumn

had been very dry; the field
went up like tinder.

Afterward there was nothing left.
You walk through it, you see nothing.

There's nothing to pick up, to smell.
The horses don't understand it—

Where is the field, they seem to say.
The way you and I would say
where is home.

No one knows how to answer them.
There is nothing left;
you have to hope, for the farmer's sake,
the insurance will pay.

It is like losing a year of your life.
To what would you lose a year of your life?

Afterward, you go back to the old place—
all that remains is char: blackness and emptiness.

You think: how could I live here?

But it was different then,
even last summer. The earth behaved

as though nothing could go wrong with it.

One match was all it took.
But at the right time—it had to be the right time.

The field parched, dry—
the deadness in place already
so to speak.

4.

I fell asleep in a river, I woke in a river,
of my mysterious
failure to die I can tell you
nothing, neither
who saved me nor for what cause—

There was immense silence.
No wind. No human sound.
The bitter century

was ended,
the glorious gone, the abiding gone,

the cold sun
persisting as a kind of curiosity, a memento,
time streaming behind it—

The sky seemed very clear,
as it is in winter,
the soil dry, uncultivated,

the official light calmly
moving through a slot in air

dignified, complacent,
dissolving hope,
subordinating images of the future to signs of the future's passing—

I think I must have fallen.
When I tried to stand, I had to force myself,
being unused to physical pain—

I had forgotten
how harsh these conditions are:

the earth not obsolete
but still, the river cold, shallow—

Of my sleep, I remember
nothing. When I cried out,
my voice soothed me unexpectedly.

In the silence of consciousness I asked myself:
why did I reject my life? And I answer
Die Erde überwältigt mich:
the earth defeats me.

I have tried to be accurate in this description
in case someone else should follow me. I can verify
that when the sun sets in winter it is
incomparably beautiful and the memory of it
lasts a long time. I think this means

there was no night.
The night was in my head.

5.

After the sun set
we rode quickly, in the hope of finding
shelter before darkness.

I could see the stars already,
first in the eastern sky:

we rode, therefore,
away from the light
and toward the sea, since
I had heard of a village there.

After some time, the snow began.
Not thickly at first, then
steadily until the earth
was covered with a white film.

The way we traveled showed
clearly when I turned my head—
for a short while it made
a dark trajectory across the earth—

Then the snow was thick, the path vanished.
The horse was tired and hungry;
he could no longer find
sure footing anywhere. I told myself:

I have been lost before, I have been cold before.
The night has come to me
exactly this way, as a premonition—

And I thought: if I am asked
to return here, I would like to come back
as a human being, and my horse

to remain himself. Otherwise
I would not know how to begin again.

A MYTH OF INNOCENCE

One summer she goes into the field as usual
stopping for a bit at the pool where she often
looks at herself, to see
if she detects any changes. She sees
the same person, the horrible mantle
of daughterliness still clinging to her.

The sun seems, in the water, very close.
That's my uncle spying again, she thinks—
everything in nature is in some way her relative.
I am never alone, she thinks,
turning the thought into a prayer.
Then death appears, like the answer to a prayer.

No one understands anymore
how beautiful he was. But Persephone remembers.
Also that he embraced her, right there,
with her uncle watching. She remembers
sunlight flashing on his bare arms.

This is the last moment she remembers clearly.
Then the dark god bore her away.

She also remembers, less clearly,
the chilling insight that from this moment
she couldn't live without him again.

The girl who disappears from the pool
will never return. A woman will return,
looking for the girl she was.

She stands by the pool saying, from time to time,
I was abducted, but it sounds
wrong to her, nothing like what she felt.
Then she says, *I was not abducted.*
Then she says, *I offered myself, I wanted*
to escape my body. Even, sometimes,
I willed this. But ignorance

cannot will knowledge. Ignorance
wills something imagined, which it believes exists.

All the different nouns—
she says them in rotation.
Death, husband, god, stranger.
Everything sounds so simple, so conventional.
I must have been, she thinks, a simple girl.

She can't remember herself as that person
but she keeps thinking the pool will remember
and explain to her the meaning of her prayer
so she can understand
whether it was answered or not.

ARCHAIC FRAGMENT

I was trying to love matter.
I taped a sign over the mirror:
You cannot hate matter and love form.

It was a beautiful day, though cold.
This was, for me, an extravagantly emotional gesture.

. . . . your poem:
tried, but could not.

I taped a sign over the first sign:
Cry, weep, thrash yourself, rend your garments—

List of things to love:
dirt, food, shells, human hair.

. . . . said
tasteless excess. Then I

rent the signs.

AIAIAIAI cried
the naked mirror.

BLUE ROTUNDA

I am tired of having hands
she said
I want wings—

But what will you do without your hands
to be human?

I am tired of human
she said
I want to live on the sun—

.

Pointing to herself:

Not here.
There is not enough
warmth in this place.
Blue sky, blue ice

the blue rotunda
lifted over
the flat street—

And then, after a silence:

.

I want
my heart back
I want to feel everything again—

That's what
the sun meant: it meant
scorched—

•

It is not finally
interesting to remember.
The damage

is not interesting.
No one who knew me then
is still alive.

My mother
was a beautiful woman—
they all said so.

•

I have to imagine
everything
she said

I have to act
as though there is actually
a map to that place:

when you were a child—

•

And then:

I'm here
because it wasn't true; I

distorted it—

•

I want she said
a theory that explains
everything

in the mother's eye
the invisible
splinter of foil

the blue ice
locked in the iris—

    .

Then:

I want it
to be my fault
she said
so I can fix it—

    .

Blue sky, blue ice,
street like a frozen river

you're talking
about my life
she said

    .

except
she said
you have to fix it

in the right order
not touching the father
until you solve the mother

.

a black space
showing
where the word ends

like a crossword saying
you should take a breath now

the black space meaning
when you were a child—

.

And then:

the ice
was there for your own protection

to teach you
not to feel—

the truth
she said

I thought it would be like
a target, you would see

the center—

.

Cold light filling the room.

I know where we are
she said
that's the window
when I was a child

That's my first home, she said
that square box—
go ahead and laugh.

Like the inside of my head:
you can see out
but you can't go out—

                     .

Just think
the sun was there, in that bare place

the winter sun
not close enough to reach
the children's hearts

the light saying
you can see out
but you can't go out

Here, it says,
here is where everything belongs

A MYTH OF DEVOTION

When Hades decided he loved this girl
he built for her a duplicate of earth,
everything the same, down to the meadow,
but with a bed added.

Everything the same, including sunlight,
because it would be hard on a young girl
to go so quickly from bright light to utter darkness.

Gradually, he thought, he'd introduce the night,
first as the shadows of fluttering leaves.
Then moon, then stars. Then no moon, no stars.
Let Persephone get used to it slowly.
In the end, he thought, she'd find it comforting.

A replica of earth
except there was love here.
Doesn't everyone want love?

He waited many years,
building a world, watching
Persephone in the meadow.
Persephone, a smeller, a taster.
If you have one appetite, he thought,
you have them all.

Doesn't everyone want to feel in the night
the beloved body, compass, polestar,
to hear the quiet breathing that says
I am alive, that means also
you are alive, because you hear me,
you are here with me. And when one turns,
the other turns—

That's what he felt, the lord of darkness,
looking at the world he had
constructed for Persephone. It never crossed his mind
that there'd be no more smelling here,
certainly no more eating.

Guilt? Terror? The fear of love?
These things he couldn't imagine;
no lover ever imagines them.

He dreams, he wonders what to call this place.
First he thinks: *The New Hell.* Then: *The Garden.*
In the end, he decides to name it
Persephone's Girlhood.

A soft light rising above the level meadow,
behind the bed. He takes her in his arms.
He wants to say *I love you, nothing can hurt you*

but he thinks
this is a lie, so he says in the end
you're dead, nothing can hurt you
which seems to him
a more promising beginning, more true.

AVERNO

You die when your spirit dies.
Otherwise, you live.
You may not do a good job of it, but you go on—
something you have no choice about.

When I tell this to my children
they pay no attention.
The old people, they think—
this is what they always do:
talk about things no one can see
to cover up all the brain cells they're losing.
They wink at each other;
listen to the old one, talking about the spirit
because he can't remember anymore the word for chair.

It is terrible to be alone.
I don't mean to live alone—
to *be* alone, where no one hears you.

I remember the word for chair.
I want to say—I'm just not interested anymore.

I wake up thinking
you have to prepare.
Soon the spirit will give up—
all the chairs in the world won't help you.

I know what they say when I'm out of the room.
Should I be seeing someone, should I be taking
one of the new drugs for depression.
I can hear them, in whispers, planning how to divide the cost.

And I want to scream out
you're all of you living in a dream.

Bad enough, they think, to watch me falling apart.
Bad enough without this lecturing they get these days
as though I had any right to this new information.

Well, they have the same right.

They're living in a dream, and I'm preparing
to be a ghost. I want to shout out

the mist has cleared—
It's like some new life:
you have no stake in the outcome;
you know the outcome.

Think of it: sixty years sitting in chairs. And now the mortal spirit
seeking so openly, so fearlessly—

To raise the veil.
To see what you're saying goodbye to.

2.

I didn't go back for a long time.
When I saw the field again, autumn was finished.
Here, it finishes almost before it starts—
the old people don't even own summer clothing.

The field was covered with snow, immaculate.
There wasn't a sign of what happened here.
You didn't know whether the farmer
had replanted or not.
Maybe he gave up and moved away.

The police didn't catch the girl.
After awhile they said she moved to some other country,
one where they don't have fields.

A disaster like this
leaves no mark on the earth.
And people like that—they think it gives them
a fresh start.

I stood a long time, staring at nothing.
After a bit, I noticed how dark it was, how cold.

A long time—I have no idea how long.
Once the earth decides to have no memory
time seems in a way meaningless.

But not to my children. They're after me
to make a will; they're worried the government
will take everything.

They should come with me sometime
to look at this field under the cover of snow.
The whole thing is written out there.

Nothing: I have nothing to give them.

That's the first part.
The second is: I don't want to be burned.

3.

On one side, the soul wanders.
On the other, human beings living in fear.
In between, the pit of disappearance.

Some young girls ask me
if they'll be safe near Averno—
they're cold, they want to go south a little while.
And one says, like a joke, but not too far south—

I say, as safe as anywhere,
which makes them happy.
What it means is nothing is safe.

You get on a train, you disappear.
You write your name on the window, you disappear.

There are places like this everywhere,
places you enter as a young girl,
from which you never return.

Like the field, the one that burned.
Afterward, the girl was gone.
Maybe she didn't exist,
we have no proof either way.

All we know is:
the field burned.
But we *saw* that.

So we have to believe in the girl,
in what she did. Otherwise
it's just forces we don't understand
ruling the earth.

The girls are happy, thinking of their vacation.
Don't take a train, I say.

They write their names in mist on a train window.
I want to say, you're good girls,
trying to leave your names behind.

4.

We spent the whole day
sailing the archipelago,
the tiny islands that were
part of the peninsula

until they'd broken off
into the fragments you see now
floating in the northern sea water.

They seemed safe to me,
I think because no one can live there.

Later we sat in the kitchen
watching the evening start and then the snow.
First one, then the other.

We grew silent, hypnotized by the snow
as though a kind of turbulence
that had been hidden before
was becoming visible,

something within the night
exposed now—

In our silence, we were asking
those questions friends who trust each other
ask out of great fatigue,
each one hoping the other knows more

and when this isn't so, hoping
their shared impressions will amount to insight.

Is there any benefit in forcing upon oneself
the realization that one must die?
Is it possible to miss the opportunity of one's life?

Questions like that.

The snow heavy. The black night
transformed into busy white air.

Something we hadn't seen revealed.
Only the meaning wasn't revealed.

5.

After the first winter, the field began to grow again.
But there were no more orderly furrows.
The smell of the wheat persisted, a kind of random aroma
intermixed with various weeds, for which
no human use has been as yet devised.

It was puzzling—no one knew
where the farmer had gone.
Some people thought he died.
Someone said he had a daughter in New Zealand,
that he went there to raise
grandchildren instead of wheat.

Nature, it turns out, isn't like us;
it doesn't have a warehouse of memory.
The field doesn't become afraid of matches,
of young girls. It doesn't remember
furrows either. It gets killed off, it gets burned,
and a year later it's alive again
as though nothing unusual has occurred.

The farmer stares out the window.
Maybe in New Zealand, maybe somewhere else.
And he thinks: *my life is over.*
His life expressed itself in that field;
he doesn't believe anymore in making anything
out of earth. The earth, he thinks,
has overpowered me.

He remembers the day the field burned,
not, he thinks, by accident.
Something deep within him said: *I can live with this,*
I can fight it after awhile.

The terrible moment was the spring after his work was erased,
when he understood that the earth
didn't know how to mourn, that it would change instead.
And then go on existing without him.

OMENS

I rode to meet you: dreams
like living beings swarmed around me
and the moon on my right side
followed me, burning.

I rode back: everything changed.
My soul in love was sad
and the moon on my left side
trailed me without hope.

To such endless impressions
we poets give ourselves absolutely,
making, in silence, omen of mere event,
until the world reflects the deepest needs of the soul.

after Alexander Pushkin

TELESCOPE

There is a moment after you move your eye away
when you forget where you are
because you've been living, it seems,
somewhere else, in the silence of the night sky.

You've stopped being here in the world.
You're in a different place,
a place where human life has no meaning.

You're not a creature in a body.
You exist as the stars exist,
participating in their stillness, their immensity.

Then you're in the world again.
At night, on a cold hill,
taking the telescope apart.

You realize afterward
not that the image is false
but the relation is false.

You see again how far away
each thing is from every other thing.

THRUSH

Snow began falling, over the surface of the whole earth.
That can't be true. And yet it felt true,
falling more and more thickly over everything I could see.
The pines turned brittle with ice.

This is the place I told you about,
where I used to come at night to see the red-winged blackbirds,
what we call *thrush* here—
red flicker of the life that disappears—

But for me—I think the guilt I feel must mean
I haven't lived very well.

Someone like me doesn't escape. I think you sleep awhile,
then you descend into the terror of the next life
except

the soul is in some different form,
more or less conscious than it was before,
more or less covetous.

After many lives, maybe something changes.
I think in the end what you want
you'll be able to see—

Then you don't need anymore
to die and come back again.

In the second version, Persephone
is dead. She dies, her mother grieves—
problems of sexuality need not
trouble us here.

Compulsively, in grief, Demeter
circles the earth. We don't expect to know
what Persephone is doing.
She is dead, the dead are mysteries.

We have here
a mother and a cipher: this is
accurate to the experience
of the mother as

she looks into the infant's face. She thinks:
I remember when you didn't exist. The infant
is puzzled; later, the child's opinion is
she has always existed, just as

her mother has always existed
in her present form. Her mother
is like a figure at a bus stop,
an audience for the bus's arrival. Before that,
she was the bus, a temporary
home or convenience. Persephone, protected,
stares out the window of the chariot.

What does she see? A morning
in early spring, in April. Now

her whole life is beginning—unfortunately,
it's going to be
a short life. She's going to know, really,

only two adults: death and her mother.
But two is
twice what her mother has:
her mother has

one child, a daughter.
As a god, she could have had
a thousand children.

We begin to see here
the deep violence of the earth

whose hostility suggests
she has no wish
to continue as a source of life.

And why is this hypothesis
never discussed? Because
it is not *in* the story; it only
creates the story.

In grief, after the daughter dies,
the mother wanders the earth.
She is preparing her case;
like a politician
she remembers everything and admits
nothing.

For example, her daughter's
birth was unbearable, her beauty
was unbearable: she remembers this.
She remembers Persephone's
innocence, her tenderness—

What is she planning, seeking her daughter?
She is issuing
a warning whose implicit message is:
what are you doing outside my body?

You ask yourself:
why is the mother's body safe?

The answer is
this is the wrong question, since

the daughter's body
doesn't exist, except
as a branch of the mother's body
that needs to be
reattached at any cost.

When a god grieves it means
destroying others (as in war)
while at the same time petitioning
to reverse agreements (as in war also):

if Zeus will get her back,
winter will end.

Winter will end, spring will return.
The small pestering breezes
that I so loved, the idiot yellow flowers—

Spring will return, a dream
based on a falsehood:
that the dead return.

Persephone
was used to death. Now over and over
her mother hauls her out again—

You must ask yourself:
are the flowers real? If

Persephone "returns" there will be
one of two reasons:

either she was not dead or
she is being used
to support a fiction—

I think I can remember
being dead. Many times, in winter,
I approached Zeus. Tell me, I would ask him,
how can I endure the earth?

And he would say,
in a short time you will be here again.
And in the time between

you will forget everything:
those fields of ice will be
the meadows of Elysium.

NOTES

"Landscape"   is for Keith Monley.

"Archaic Fragment"   is for Dana Levin.

"Thrush"   is for Noah Max Horwitz and
Susan Kimmelman, in memory.